COMMON CORE CLINICS

Grade 8

CLINICS

English Language Arts

Reading Informational Text

ommon Core Clinics, English Language Arts, Reading Informational Text, Grade 8

T271 / 383NA

SBN-13: 978-0-7836-8486-4

over Image: © fStop/Alamy

riumph Learning® 136 Madison Avenue, 7th Floor, New York, NY 10016

2012 Triumph Learning, LLC
oach is an imprint of Triumph Learning®

rinted in the United States of America.

0 9 8 7 6 5 4

ALL ABOUT YOUR BOOK

COMMON CORE CLINICS will help you master important reading skills.

Each lesson has a **Learn About It** box that teaches the idea. A sample passage focuses on the skill. A **graphic organizer** shows you a reading strategy.

Each lesson has a **Try It** passage with **guided reading**.

HOTS Higher-Order Thinking Skills

Questions that make you think further about what you read.

Apply It provides **independent practice** for reading passages, answering short-answer questions, and responding to writing prompts.

Table of Contents

Main Idea and Supporting Details

Learn About It

The **main idea** of a passage is the overall message that its author is trying to convey. The main idea is sometimes found at the beginning or end of passages, but this is not always the case. In fact, sometimes the main idea is not even stated directly in the text. To find the main idea, look for links between the **details** given in the passage, and try to identify recurring phrases or ideas. Also, pay special attention to sentences that include **transition words** such as *thus, therefore, however,* and *in conclusion,* as these often point to the main idea of a passage.

Read the passage. As you read, pay attention to recurring phrases or ideas to help you determine the main idea.

For decades, testing medicine on animals was considered an effective way of predicting how humans would react to these medicines. However, recent evidence shows that humans are not as physiologically similar to other mammals as was once thought. For example, studies have shown that certain substances that are harmful to lab mice have little or no effect on humans, and vice versa.

Supporting Details	Recurring Ideas/Links	Main Idea
Animal testing once thought to be effective New evidence shows that animals and humans are not similar Substances have different effects on humans and animals	Animals Humans Medicine testing New evidence/studies Different results	Testing medicine on animals is not as effective as it was once thought to be.

Try It

Read the passage. As you read, circle any recurring words, phrases, or ideas to help you identify the main idea. Use the questions to help you.

excerpted and adapted from

The Gospel of Wealth
by Andrew Carnegie

In bestowing charity, the main consideration should be to help those who will help themselves; to provide part of the means by which those who desire to improve may do so; to give those who desire to use the aids by which they may rise; to assist, but rarely or never to do all. Neither the individual nor the race is improved by mere alms-giving. The only true reformer is he who is as careful and as anxious not to aid the unworthy as he is to aid the worthy, and, perhaps, even more so, for in alms-giving more injury is probably done by rewarding vice than by relieving virtue.

> What ideas or themes are repeated throughout the passage?

The best means of benefiting the community is to place within its reach the ladders upon which the aspiring can rise—parks, and means of recreation, by which men are helped in body and mind; works of art, certain to give pleasure and improve the public taste, and public institutions of various kinds, which will improve the general condition of the people—in this manner returning their surplus wealth to the mass of their fellows in the forms best calculated to do them lasting good.

Thus is the problem of rich and poor to be solved. The laws of accumulation will be left free; the laws of distribution free. Individualism will continue, but the millionaire will be but a trustee for the poor; entrusted for a season with a great part of the increased wealth of the community, but administering it for the community far better than it could or would have done for itself. The best minds will thus have reached a stage in the development of the race in which it is clearly seen that there is no mode of disposing of surplus wealth creditable to thoughtful and earnest men into whose hands it flows save by using it year by year for the general good.

Continued on the next page

Continued from the previous page

This day already dawns. But a little while, and although, without incurring the pity of their fellows, men may die sharers in great business enterprises from which their capital cannot be or has not been withdrawn, and is left chiefly at death for public uses. Yet the man who dies leaving behind many millions of available wealth, which was his to administer during life, will pass away "unwept, unhonored, and unsung," no matter to what uses he leaves the inheritance which he cannot take with him. Of such as these the public verdict will then be: "The man who dies thus rich dies disgraced."

Such, in my opinion, is the true Gospel concerning Wealth, obedience to which is destined some day to solve the problem of the rich and the poor, and to bring "Peace on earth, among men Good-Will."

> **What type of people does Carnegie believe will be "unwept, unhonored, and unsung"?**

> **What details can you find that support the main idea?**

HOTS Analyze

The words *charity*, *rise*, *wealth*, and *community* are mentioned several times in this passage. From this, what can you conclude about the main idea of the passage?

Apply It

Read the passage. As you read, pay attention to recurring ideas or phrases to help you identify the main idea. Answer the questions that follow.

Theodore Roosevelt

As evidenced by the fact that he is immortalized in stone alongside Washington, Jefferson, and Lincoln, Theodore Roosevelt is one of our most revered presidents, and in polls taken since the middle of the twentieth century, he often ranks among the top five most popular. The youngest man to ever hold the office, Roosevelt helped set the course for American politics in the twentieth century, and embodied the bold, adventurous spirit that helped elevate the United States to the level of world superpower. While his impact on American government is well documented, what is often overlooked is the way Roosevelt influenced the way Americans speak English. Phrases that he coined or inspired continue to pepper our speech almost a century after he left office. Many of his sayings are so common and universal in their application that many have forgotten that they had any connection to Roosevelt in the first place.

Few people realize, for example, that the Teddy in the term "teddy bear" is a direct reference to Roosevelt himself. The term is derived from an incident that occurred during a bear hunt that Roosevelt attended with Mississippi governor Andrew Longino in 1902. During that hunt, Roosevelt refused to kill a black bear that had been trapped and tied up by a group of his attendants; he deemed such an action unsportsmanlike. A cartoon accompanying newspaper accounts of the story depicted the great bear as a small, cuddly cub, and the anecdote and the cartoon image soon spread across the country. A toy manufacturer was so inspired by the tale that he created a plush bear based on the cartoon image, and received Roosevelt's permission to attach the president's nickname to his creation. Within a few years, the teddy bear became a worldwide hit, and has remained a staple of childhood bedrooms ever since.

Roosevelt also originated the term "bully pulpit," which has come to mean a position of authority that gives its holder broad powers to shape public discourse and influence policy. Roosevelt first coined the term during a White House meeting with his advisors. While reviewing one of his upcoming speeches, Roosevelt tried to gauge what his critic's reaction might be. He then exclaimed, "I suppose my critics will call that preaching, but I've got such a bully pulpit!" The quote was picked up by the *New York Times*, and it quickly became a part of public language. Over the years, the term has grown to have something of a pejorative meaning; many equate the term "bully" with its modern connotation of aggressiveness or harassment. It should be noted Roosevelt was using the term in its original sense, which means something closer to "excellent."

Continued on the next page ➤

Continued from the previous page

The list of Roosevelt's linguistic innovations—*lunatic fringe, square deal, big stick policy*—goes on and on. Like his image on Mt. Rushmore, they stand as a living monument to the enduring influence he continues to have on American life.

Answer these questions about "Theodore Roosevelt." Write your answers in complete sentences.

1. One student who studied this passage concluded that its main idea is "Theodore Roosevelt is one of our greatest presidents." How do you think this student reached this conclusion?

   _____

   _____

2. What is the main idea of the second paragraph?

   _____

   _____

3. What is the main idea of the third paragraph?

   _____

   _____

4. What themes or ideas are common to both the second and third paragraphs?

   _____

   _____

5. Based on your answer to the previous question, what is the main idea of this passage?

   _____

   _____

Summarize Text

Learn About It

Summarizing a text involves recalling the main points of a passage. A summary is a restatement of the main idea as well as a general overview of the supporting details used in a passage. In other words, a summary is a brief description of *what* the author says and *how* the author says it. To summarize a text, carefully read the passage and make sure you understand the main idea of each paragraph, and take note of recurring ideas or supporting details. Then, form one or two sentences that describe how these elements relate to one another.

Read the passage. After you have read, use the graphic organizer below to help you create a summary of the passage.

To improve our nation's overall health, our government should impose a higher tax on the purchase of candy. Such a tax might discourage people from eating candy, which would lead to a decrease in health issues such as diabetes. In addition, the added revenue generated by this tax could be used to fund health education programs in our public schools.

Main Idea
A higher tax on candy would improve the nation's health.

Detail	**Detail**	**Detail**
A higher tax might discourage people from buying candy.	Discouraging people from eating candy may reduce the amount of diabetes.	Higher tax revenue can fund health programs in public schools.

Try It

Read the passage. As you read, circle the main idea and underline the supporting details of each paragraph. Use the questions to help you.

Texting and Driving

In many ways, the invention of the cellular phone has been a great boon to travelers. It has allowed drivers who are stranded to instantly phone for help without leaving their cars, and to alert the police and other authorities to dangerous road conditions and emergencies. However, these benefits are overshadowed by the dangers that come from drivers choosing to use their cell phones while in the act of driving. As the percentage of people using cell phones has skyrocketed over the past twenty years, authorities have noticed an accompanying rise in the number of cell-phone-related accidents.

> What course of action does the author of this passage recommend?

This has been especially true since the advent of texting, a process that allows cell phone users to transmit short, typed messages to one another. Texting has proven to be a remarkably convenient method of communication, and as a result, it has also become wildly popular. According to recent estimates, over 110 *billion* text messages are sent each month in the United States alone. The problem is that since texting has become so convenient and widespread, most users have come to believe that they can text while performing other operations that require their full attention and coordination. And driving is just such an activity. In a growing number of cases, the mixture of texting and driving has proven deadly: statistics have shown that up to sixteen percent of all traffic fatalities last year were texting-related.

> What evidence does the author present to support this recommendation?

While most "professional" texters would argue that they can text almost as easily as they can talk, studies have shown that even the most casual text involves a number of processes that can seriously impede a motorist's ability to react in a time of emergency. First, and most obviously, texting requires that the driver devote at least one hand to the cell phone's keypad, thus limiting the driver's ability to control the vehicle.

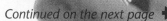

ttyl. i'm driving

Continued on the next page ➔

Continued from the previous page

More importantly, a person who composes a text spends an average of five seconds looking at the cell phone's display screen. Five seconds might not seem like that much time, but when driving, it can mean the difference between stopping just short of an accident and being the cause of one. A recent closed-course test found that subjects who composed or read texts when driving took four times as long to react to accident scenarios as those who were not texting. Their reaction times were even worse than those of drivers under the influence of alcohol.

What are the most important details in this passage?

Many cell phone users might argue that the use of a hands-free device eliminates the dangers of using a cell phone while driving. But in fact, those who texted using a voice-activated texting system in the study mentioned above fared just as poorly as their hands-on counterparts. This is because while such hands-free devices might allow drivers to use both hands while driving, the simple act of talking on the phone deprives them of something just as important: concentration. In light of all of this evidence, it is clear that, in the interest of public safety, all states should criminalize driving "under the influence" of cell phones.

What is the main idea of this passage?

HOTS Analyze

Summarize the passage. How does summarizing the passage help you understand it?

Apply It

Read the passage. As you read, pay attention to the main idea and supporting details of each paragraph. Answer the questions that follow.

Healthy Solutions

Childhood obesity is a serious medical condition that affects children and adolescents, and in recent years, the percentage of young people whose body weight index classifies them as obese has risen dramatically. According to a recent study, almost seventeen percent of American children are obese—three times as many as in the 1970s. As such, childhood obesity has become a national concern, not only because it causes low self-esteem and depression in young adults, but also because it leads to serious health problems that carry into adulthood, such as diabetes, high blood pressure, and high cholesterol. To combat this problem, the federal government has partnered with professional sports organizations in a nationwide campaign to encourage children to adopt better eating and exercise habits earlier in life. Such efforts will definitely have a pronounced impact, but there are also a number of policies we can enact on a local level to pitch in and do our part.

The first step involves taking action in our public schools. We can start by removing vending machines that sell soda and candy from our school hallways. The snacks these machines dispense are high in sugar, caffeine, and calories, and very low in nutritional

value. In their place, we can encourage schools to grant students expanded access to their cafeterias throughout the school day, where they can purchase healthier foods such as fruits, vegetables, and snacks made from whole grains. In addition, we should press to make physical education a larger part of our curriculum, and mandate that students spend a certain amount of each school day involved in some sort of rigorous physical exercise.

At the same time, we should put pressure on local fast food franchises to curtail their advertising efforts aimed at children. Fast food advertisers have long known that when children become attracted to a particular brand at a young age, they usually remain loyal customers well into adulthood. As a result, they often use images of cuddly animals and colorful cartoons when pitching their products to youngsters.

Continued on the next page ➤

Continued from the previous page

Some chains even offer toys with their "children's meals" in order to lure in pint-sized customers. Parents who succumb to pressure to get their child that "must-have" toy often do not realize that in some cases, the one meal attached to that toy contains over half the amount of calories a child should consume in an entire day. While it might seem excessive to go so far as to ban such advertising, advertisers must be made to account for their role in what is fast becoming a national health crisis.

Parents, for their part, need to lead by example and make exercising and eating healthily a family affair. Studies have shown that children who share at least one nutritious meal a day with their families not only eat better, but communicate more effectively and perform better in school. By just setting aside a bit of time for exercise and healthy eating each day, we can help our children live longer, healthier, happier lives.

Answer these questions about "Healthy Solutions." Write your answers in complete sentences.

1. What is the main idea of the first paragraph?

_____

_____

2. What does the author recommend in the second paragraph?

_____

_____

3. How does the third paragraph contribute to the author's argument?

_____

_____

4. What is the author's conclusion?

_____

_____

5. Based on your answers to the preceding questions, write a short summary of the passage.

_____

_____

_____

_____

Analyze Connections and Distinctions

Learn About It

In order to illustrate a claim or support an argument, authors will often make connections or distinctions between different people, ideas, institutions, or events. Authors can clarify a statement regarding a subject by showing how it is similar to another subject through the use of **comparisons** or **analogies**. For example, if an author wanted to argue that a person is an effective leader, he or she could do so by demonstrating how this person resembles another effective leader. Authors often organize objects, ideas, or events into different **categories** to make comparing or contrasting them easier.

Read the passage. As you read, take note of how the author makes use of connections, distinctions, and categories in the passage.

Though they both crawl on the ground and are incorrectly labeled as pests by most people, spiders are not the same as insects. Insects, by definition, have a head, thorax, abdomen, and six legs. Spiders, on the other hand, have eight legs, and have bodies that are divided into only two segments. Therefore, spiders and insects belong to different orders in the animal kingdom.

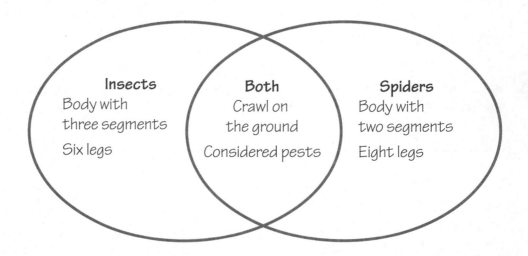

Insects
Body with three segments
Six legs

Both
Crawl on the ground
Considered pests

Spiders
Body with two segments
Eight legs

Try It

Read the passage. As you read, circle things the author compares to each other. Use the questions to help you.

Our Founders and Ancient Rome

To appreciate the tremendous influence that the civilization of ancient Rome continues to have on American society, all you need to do is take a tour of our nation's capital. Most of its architectural flourishes—from the dome of the Capitol building to the columns of the Supreme Court—look as though they were copied directly from the ruins of the old Roman Forum. But look more closely and you will see that Rome's most enduring legacy lies not in these structures, but rather in the institutions that are housed within them.

> The author shows connections between the United States and ancient Rome in both government and architecture.

Raised on the works of Latin authors such as Virgil, Plutarch, and Cicero, our country's founders grew up with a deep reverence for Roman ideas and institutions, and in many ways viewed themselves as modern versions of their old Roman heroes. So it was only natural that when it came time for the founders to form their own government, they should pattern it after that of their idols. Before it was ruled by emperors, Rome was organized as a republic. A republic is a system of government in which elected officials carry out the business of the state and are accountable to the people who elect them. Rome's republic was guided by a written law code known as the Law of the Twelve Tables, which is in many ways a precursor to our American Constitution. The ancient Romans, like the founders, recognized that a written law code was necessary to clearly define the powers of government and protect the rights of its citizens.

One of the most important ideas that the founders borrowed from their Roman forebearers was the principle that power should be divided between different branches of government. Under the Roman republican system, executive authority was wielded by two elected consuls, who can be thought of as co-presidents. These consuls were in charge of the Roman military, and were responsible for shaping civic policy. The Roman Senate worked in partnership with two lower assemblies to draft legislation, control financial affairs, and manage foreign policy.

> What link does the author make between the founders and Latin authors? How is this link relevant?

Perhaps the greatest innovation of the Roman republic was a system of checks and balances that was designed to ensure that none of these different branches grew more powerful than the others. For example, consuls controlled Rome's armies, but were subject to strict one-year term limits. Since the Senate controlled the state's finances, consuls had to rely on the Senate's support to have their policies enacted.

Continued on the next page ➡

Continued from the previous page

Senators held office for life, but any action of the Senate could be cancelled by a veto from either one of the two sitting consuls.

The founders, who had just freed themselves from what they viewed as a tyrannical system, found this aspect of Roman government particularly appealing, and they inserted similar stopgaps into their own Constitution. For example, the American president serves as commander-in-chief of the armed forces, but Congress controls the finances that, among other things, fund the armed forces. Only Congress has the power to initiate legislation, but its acts can be delayed or nullified by a presidential veto.

How does the example of the Law of the Twelve Tables strengthen the author's argument?

How does the Roman Senate compare to the United States Congress?

HOTS Evaluate

How do analogies and direct comparisons help to strengthen the author's argument?

Apply It

Read the passage. As you read, pay attention to how connections and categories help strengthen the author's argument. Answer the questions that follow.

Birds and Dinosaurs

Where do birds come from? A simple, flippant response might be "eggs" or "the sky," but the real answer might actually surprise you. An ever-increasing body of scientific evidence suggests that birds are, in fact, the distant cousins of dinosaurs. While some scientists still dispute this link, recent fossil studies have shown that in regard to their external characteristics, skeletal structures, and breathing systems, birds resemble dinosaurs more closely than any other animal group. By studying the similarities between these fossils and modern birds, scientists are learning a great deal about how dinosaurs lived and acted, and how birds evolved into their present form.

Most people are unaware that birds are, technically speaking, reptiles, and as such, belong to the same class of animals to which dinosaurs belong. In terms of soft anatomy—that is, musculature, brain, and internal organs—birds and reptiles are remarkably similar to one another. Their reproductive systems are also similar.

Continued on the next page ➤

Continued from the previous page

Like birds, reptiles reproduce by laying eggs. The tissues that produce a bird's feathers resemble those that produce scales in reptiles—scales that are clearly visible on a bird's feet. (If you were to compare the scaly talons of an ostrich or an emu to those of a crocodile or lizard, the link would become even more obvious.) In fact, as a result of recent fossil discoveries in China, scientists now know that some small dinosaurs that did not fly had feathers. This has led many to theorize that feathers were initially designed not for flight, but for warmth.

Another feature of birds that was previously thought to have developed specifically for flight is their light, hollow bone structure. Scientists have noticed the same trait in the remains of flightless dinosaurs, which has led them to conclude that this type of skeletal structure must have initially developed for some other purpose. The most likely explanation seems to be that its original purpose was not to enable flight, but to facilitate respiration.

Birds do not possess lungs that operate like those of humans or other vertebrates. Rather, they possess a highly efficient system of air sacs in their bones that regulates their respiration, allowing fresh air to constantly circulate through their bodies. Once again, it was previously thought that this breathing system was an evolutionary feature specifically developed to enable flight. However, new studies have shown that flightless dinosaurs, such as the great *Tyrannosaurus rex*, had a similar breathing system. This discovery has led scientists to speculate that this breathing system was initially developed to allow cold-blooded animals such as dinosaurs to store and use energy more efficiently. This would have allowed predatory dinosaurs such as the *T. rex* to remain more active over longer stretches of time. Modern reptiles that have this respiratory system are forced to remain relatively inactive in order to conserve energy.

The fact that two seemingly different species, separated by millions of years of evolutionary history, resemble each other so closely has led scientists to reevaluate previously held assumptions regarding evolution. They have now come to believe that evolution is not a system of smooth transitions between closely related species. Rather, it is a series of fits and starts, in which physiological features are adapted and then re-adapted to meet changing environmental realities.

Answer these questions about "Birds and Dinosaurs." Write your answers in complete sentences.

1. How does the author establish a link between birds and reptiles in this passage?

_____

_____

2. How is the author able to use the link between birds and reptiles to make a connection between birds and dinosaurs?

_____

_____

3. What role does fossil evidence play in the author's argument?

_____

_____

4. How does the author's analysis of breathing structures support the main idea of the passage?

_____

_____

Drawing and Supporting Inferences

Learn About It

An **inference** is a **conclusion** based on the facts presented in a passage. Such conclusions are not stated directly by the author. Rather, it is left up to readers to draw their own inferences by comparing the information presented in a passage with their own personal experience and knowledge.

Read the passage. As you read, use your own personal experience to draw inferences from the facts given in the text.

Hosni Mubarak became the leader of Egypt in 1981. He stayed in power for thirty years. In January 2011, many Egyptian citizens protested against Mubarak's regime and fought for a democratic form of government.

What I Read	What I Know	My Inference
Hosni Mubarak was the leader of Egypt for thirty years. Egyptian citizens revolted against his leadership. The citizens fought for a democratic government.	When people are not happy, they demand change. American colonists in the 18th century fought against a monarchy.	The Egyptian people were not happy with Mubarak's government because it was not democratic.

Try It

Read the passage. As you read, combine the facts presented in the passage with your own personal experience and knowledge of history to make inferences about its meaning. Use the questions to help you.

On the day following the Japanese attack on Pearl Harbor, U.S. President Franklin Delano Roosevelt delivered the following speech to a joint session of Congress.

Yesterday, December 7th, 1941—a date which will live in infamy—the United States of America was suddenly and deliberately attacked by naval and air forces of the Empire of Japan.

The United States was at peace with that nation and, at the solicitation of Japan, was still in conversation with its government and its emperor looking toward the maintenance of peace in the Pacific.

Indeed, one hour after Japanese air squadrons had commenced bombing in the American island of Oahu, the Japanese ambassador to the United States and his colleague delivered to our Secretary of State a formal reply to a recent American message. And while this reply stated that it seemed useless to continue the existing diplomatic negotiations, it contained no threat or hint of war or of armed attack.

It will be recorded that the distance of Hawaii from Japan makes it obvious that the attack was deliberately planned many days or even weeks ago. During the intervening time, the Japanese government has deliberately sought to deceive the United States by false statements and expressions of hope for continued peace.

> **What information given in the fourth paragraph allowed Roosevelt to infer that Japan's attack was premeditated?**

The attack yesterday on the Hawaiian islands has caused severe damage to American naval and military forces. I regret to tell you that very many American lives have been lost. In addition, American ships have been reported torpedoed on the high seas between San Francisco and Honolulu.

Yesterday, the Japanese government also launched an attack against Malaya. Last night, Japanese forces attacked Hong Kong. Last night, Japanese forces attacked Guam. Last night, Japanese forces attacked the Philippine Islands.

> **Consider the information given in the sixth paragraph, and the conclusion Roosevelt draws in the seventh paragraph. What inference can you make regarding the relationship between these territories and the United States?**

Continued on the next page ➡

Continued from the previous page

Last night, the Japanese attacked Wake Island. And this morning, the Japanese attacked Midway Island.

Japan has, therefore, undertaken a surprise offensive extending throughout the Pacific area. The facts of yesterday and today speak for themselves. The people of the United States have already formed their opinions and well understand the implications to the very life and safety of our nation.

> **Why do you think Japan attacked all those islands in the Pacific Ocean at the same time?**

As commander-in-chief of the Army and Navy, I have directed that all measures be taken for our defense. But always will our whole nation remember the character of the onslaught against us.

No matter how long it may take us to overcome this premeditated invasion, the American people in their righteous might will win through to absolute victory.

I believe that I interpret the will of the Congress and of the people when I assert that we will not only defend ourselves to the uttermost, but will make it very certain that this form of treachery shall never again endanger us.

Hostilities exist. There is no blinking at the fact that our people, our territory, and our interests are in grave danger.

With confidence in our armed forces, with the unbounding determination of our people, we will gain the inevitable triumph. . .

> **How do you think American citizens reacted to the bombing of Pearl Harbor?**

I ask that the Congress declare that since the unprovoked and dastardly attack by Japan on Sunday, December 7th, 1941, a state of war has existed between the United States and the Japanese empire.

HOTS Analyze

Roosevelt points out that Japan attacked the United States while the two countries were in diplomatic negotiations. Judging from his reaction, what can you infer about the legitimacy of such an action?

Apply It

Read the passage. As you read, use evidence from the passage and what you know to draw and support inferences. Answer the questions that follow.

excerpted and adapted from
Life on the Mississippi
by Mark Twain

The Mississippi is well worth reading about. It is not a commonplace river, but on the contrary is in all ways remarkable. Considering the Missouri its main branch, it is the longest river in the world—four thousand three hundred miles. It seems safe to say that it is also the crookedest river in the world, since in one part of its journey it uses up one thousand three hundred miles to cover the same ground that the crow would fly over in six hundred and seventy-five. It discharges three times as much water as the St. Lawrence, twenty-five times as much as the Rhine, and three hundred and thirty-eight times as much as the Thames. No other river has so vast a drainage-basin: it draws its water supply from twenty-eight States and Territories; from Delaware, on the Atlantic seaboard, and from all the country between that and Idaho on the Pacific slope—a spread of forty-five degrees of longitude. The Mississippi receives and carries to the Gulf water from fifty-four subordinate rivers that are navigable by steamboats, and from some hundreds that are navigable by flats and keels. The area of its drainage-basin is as great as the combined areas of England, Wales, Scotland, Ireland, France, Spain, Portugal, Germany, Austria, Italy, and Turkey; and almost all this wide region is fertile; the Mississippi valley, proper, is exceptionally so.

Continued on the next page ➡

Continued from the previous page

It is a remarkable river in this: that instead of widening toward its mouth, it grows narrower; grows narrower and deeper. From the junction of the Ohio to a point half way down to the sea, the width averages a mile in high water: thence to the sea the width steadily diminishes, until, at the 'Passes,' above the mouth, it is but little over half a mile. At the junction of the Ohio the Mississippi's depth is eighty-seven feet; the depth increases gradually, reaching one hundred and twenty-nine just above the mouth.

The difference in rise and fall is also remarkable—not in the upper, but in the lower river. The rise is tolerably uniform down to Natchez (three hundred and sixty miles above the mouth)—about fifty feet. But at Bayou La Fourche the river rises only twenty-four feet; at New Orleans only fifteen, and just above the mouth only two and one half.

The mud deposit gradually extends the land—but only gradually; it has extended it not quite a third of a mile in the two hundred years which have elapsed since the river took its place in history. The belief of the scientific people is that the mouth used to be at Baton Rouge, where the hills cease, and that the two hundred miles of land between there and the Gulf was built by the river. This gives us the age of that piece of country, without any trouble at all—one hundred and twenty thousand years. Yet it is much the youthfullest batch of country that lies around there anywhere.

Answer these questions about "Life on the Mississippi." Write your answers in complete sentences.

1. Judging from the information given in the first paragraph, what can you infer about the shape of most rivers in the world?

   _____

   _____

2. If a river were discovered that drew its water supply from over thirty states and territories, what might you be able to infer about its drainage basin?

   _____

   _____

3. Based on the information given in the second paragraph, what can you infer about what happens to most rivers as you approach their "mouths"?

   _____

   _____

4. Based on the information given in the third paragraph, what can you infer about the "rise and fall" of most rivers?

   _____

   _____

5. In the last paragraph, what is the author able to infer from the fact that "the two hundred miles between there and the Gulf was built by the river"?

   _____

   _____

Supporting an Analysis of a Text

Learn About It

Analyzing a work of **nonfiction** involves breaking a text down into its different parts to determine what an author is trying to say, and then judging how effectively he or she conveys this message. Study the overall structure of a passage, examine the author's use of language, and **evaluate** the strength and relevance of the author's evidence. In many cases, the proper analysis of a passage also involves expanding upon what the text says by **drawing conclusions** or **making inferences** based on the information provided.

Read the quote from Thomas Jefferson. As you read, take note of the different elements of nonfiction.

A book is not a frivolous expense—it is a sound investment. A library book can last as long as a house, for hundreds of years. The knowledge it imparts last even longer. It is not, then, an article of mere consumption but rather a source of wealth, and often in the case of young people, setting out in life, it is the only wealth they will ever need.

Nonfiction Elements to Analyze		
Structure	**Language**	**Argument**
Main idea	Author's word choice and tone	Author's purpose and point of view
Supporting details	Figurative language	Author's evidence
Paragraph organization		Connections to other texts or ideas
Type of media used		Responses to conflicting texts or evidence

Try It

Read the passage. As you read, pay attention to the structure, language, and arguments used in the passage. Use the questions to help you.

The following is excerpted and adapted from one of the letters of Benjamin Franklin, dated January 26, 1784. In it, he discusses his feelings regarding the appropriateness of the bald eagle as a national symbol, and argues in favor of using what he considers a more appropriate bird.

Some have expressed their displeasure that the bald eagle has been chosen for our new nation's emblem, objecting to it as looking too much like a *dindon*, or turkey. For my own part, I wish the bald eagle had not been chosen as the representative of our country; he is a bird of bad moral character; he does not get his living honestly; you may have seen him perched on some dead tree, where, too lazy to fish for himself, he watches the labor of the fishing-hawk; and, when that diligent bird has at length taken a fish, and is bearing it to his nest for the support of his mate and young ones, the bald eagle pursues him, and takes it from him. With all this injustice he is never in good case; but, like those among men who live by sharping and robbing, he is generally poor, and often very lousy. Besides, he is a rank coward; the little kingbird, not bigger than a sparrow, attacks him boldly and drives him out of the district. He is therefore by no means a proper emblem for the brave and honest Cincinnati of America, who have driven all the kingbirds from our country; though exactly fit for that order of knights, which the French call *Chevaliers d'Industrie*.

> What sort of evidence does Franklin use to argue against using the bald eagle as a symbol?

> Does Franklin give a convincing argument against the bald eagle? Are there any details you feel he could have added?

Continued on the next page ➡

Continued from the previous page

I am, on this account, not displeased that the figure is not known as a bald eagle, but looks more like a turkey. For in truth, the turkey is in comparison a much more respectable bird, and withal a true original native of America. Eagles have been found in all countries, but the turkey was peculiar to ours; the first of the species seen in Europe, being brought to France by the Jesuits from Canada, and served up at the wedding table of Charles the Ninth. He is, besides, (though a little vain and silly, it is true, but not the worse emblem for that,) a bird of courage, and would not hesitate to attack a grenadier of the British guards, who should presume to invade his farmyard with a red coat on.

> **Why does Franklin feel that the turkey would be a better symbol?**

HOTS Analyze

How does Franklin make use of figurative language to strengthen his argument?

Apply It

Read the passage. As you read, pay attention to how the author makes use of the different elements of nonfiction. Answer the questions that follow.

excerpted and adapted from

The Declaration of Sentiments
by Elizabeth Cady Stanton

When, in the course of human events, it becomes necessary for one portion of the family of man to assume among the people of the earth a position different from that which they have hitherto occupied, but one to which the laws of nature and of nature's God entitle them, a decent respect to the opinions of mankind requires that they should declare the causes that impel them to such a course.

We hold these truths to be self-evident: that all men and women are created equal; that they are endowed by their Creator with certain inalienable rights; that among these are life, liberty, and the pursuit of happiness; that to secure these rights governments are instituted, deriving their just powers from the consent of the governed. Whenever any form of government becomes destructive of these ends, it is the right of those who suffer from it to refuse allegiance to it, and to insist upon the institution of a new government, laying its foundation on such principles, and organizing its powers in such form, as to them shall seem most likely to effect their safety and happiness. Prudence, indeed, will dictate that governments long established should not be changed for light and transient causes; and accordingly all experience has shown that mankind are more disposed to suffer, while evils are sufferable, than to right themselves by abolishing the forms to which they are accustomed.

But when a long train of abuses and usurpations, pursuing invariably the same object, evinces a design to reduce them under absolute despotism, it is their duty to throw off such government, and to provide new guards for their future security. Such has been the patient sufferance of the women under this government, and such is now the necessity which constrains them to demand the equal station to which they are entitled.

Continued on the next page ➡

Continued from the previous page

The history of mankind is a history of repeated injuries and usurpations on the part of man toward woman, having in direct object the establishment of an absolute tyranny over her. To prove this, let facts be submitted to a candid world.

He has never permitted her to exercise her inalienable right to the elective franchise.

He has compelled her to submit to laws, in the formation of which she had no voice.

He has withheld from her rights which are given to the most ignorant and degraded men—both natives and foreigners.

Having deprived her of this first right of a citizen, the elective franchise, thereby leaving her without representation in the halls of legislation, he has oppressed her on all sides.

He has taken from her all right in property, even to the wages she earns.

Now, in view of this entire disfranchisement of one-half the people of this country, their social and religious degradation—in view of the unjust laws above mentioned, and because women do feel themselves aggrieved, oppressed, and fraudulently deprived of their most sacred rights, we insist that they have immediate admission to all the rights and privileges which belong to them as citizens of the United States.

Answer these questions about "The Declaration of Sentiments." Write your answers in complete sentences.

1. What is the main idea of this passage?

_____

_____

2. What evidence does the author offer to support her position?

_____

_____

3. From the information provided, what can you infer about the state of women's rights at the time the passage was written?

_____

_____

4. In form and tone, what other famous "Declaration" does this passage resemble?

_____

_____

5. Why do you think the author chose to make such a connection between her text and the other declaration?

_____

_____

_____

_____

Figurative, Connotative, and Technical Meanings

Learn About It

Words can have figurative, connotative, or technical meanings. To make their writing more expressive and interesting, authors will often use **figurative language**. This literary device involves using words in ways that go beyond their literal, dictionary definitions. One of the most common uses of figurative language is a **metaphor**, which is a direct comparison between two unlike things. **Connotation** is an implied meaning or an emotional weight a word carries. Some nonfiction is **technical** and uses words specific to a particular topic, such as computer terms.

Read the passage. As you read, pay attention to the author's use of language.

A pedometer is a device used to count the number of steps you take. It is about the same size as a cellular phone. You wear it on your belt or place it in a front pocket in line with the middle of your leg. Inside the pedometer is a tiny spring-set horizontal arm. The arm moves up and down each time you take a step. Each step is counted when an electrical circuit senses the movements of your pelvis.

Technical Words	Meanings
Pedometer	Step counter
Device	Tool
Cellular	Wireless
Electrical circuit	Path
Pelvis	Hips

Try It

Read the passage. As you read, underline any figurative language. Use the questions to help you.

The following is an excerpt from a speech given by former British Prime Minister Winston Churchill at Westminster College in Fulton, Missouri, on March 5, 1946.

A shadow has fallen upon the scenes so lately lighted by the Allied victory. Nobody knows what Soviet Russia and its Communist international organization intends to do in the immediate future, or what are the limits, if any, to their expansive… tendencies. I have a strong admiration and regard for the valiant Russian people and for my wartime comrade, Marshal Stalin. There is deep sympathy and goodwill in Britain—and I doubt not here also—towards the peoples of all the Russias and a resolve to persevere through many differences and rebuffs in establishing lasting friendships. We understand the Russian need to be secure on her western frontiers by the removal of all possibility of German aggression. We welcome Russia to her rightful place among the leading nations of the world. We welcome her flag upon the seas. Above all, we welcome constant, frequent and growing contacts between the Russian people and our own people on both sides of the Atlantic. It is my duty however, for I am sure you would wish me to state the facts as I see them to you, to place before you certain facts about the present position in Europe.

> **What is the connotative meaning of the word *shadow* as it is used in the first paragraph?**

> **When Churchill says that "we welcome her flag upon the seas" in the first paragraph, what do you think he means?**

From Stettin in the Baltic to Trieste in the Adriatic, an iron curtain has descended across the continent. Behind that line lie all the capitals of the ancient states of Central and Eastern Europe. Warsaw, Berlin, Prague, Vienna, Budapest, Belgrade, Bucharest and Sofia, all these famous cities and the populations around them lie in what I must call the Soviet sphere, and all are subject in one form or another, not only to Soviet influence but to a very high and, in some cases, increasing measure of control from Moscow. Athens alone—Greece with its immortal glories—is free to decide its future at an election under British, American, and French observation.

Continued on the next page ▶

Continued from the previous page

The Russian-dominated Polish government has been encouraged to make enormous and wrongful inroads upon Germany, and mass expulsions of millions of Germans on a scale grievous and undreamed-of are now taking place. The Communist parties, which were very small in all these eastern states of Europe, have been raised to preeminence and power far beyond their numbers and are seeking everywhere to obtain totalitarian control. Police governments are prevailing in nearly every case, and so far, except in Czechoslovakia, there is no true democracy.

> **How is the word *sphere* used in this passage? How does this use differ from its mathematical meaning?**

If now the Soviet government tries, by separate action, to build up a pro-Communist Germany in their areas, this will cause new serious difficulties in the American and British zones, and will give the defeated Germans the power of putting themselves up to auction between the Soviets and the Western democracies. Whatever conclusions may be drawn from these facts—and facts they are—this is certainly not the liberated Europe we fought to build up. Nor is it one which contains the essentials of permanent peace.

> **What are communism and democracy? What is the connotation of each one?**

HOTS Analyze

What is the meaning of Churchill's "iron curtain" metaphor?

Apply It

Read the passage. As you read, pay attention how the author makes use of the meanings of technical terms. Answer the questions that follow.

The Electric Guitar

The largest part of an electric guitar is known as the **body**. For right-handed players, the body rests on the player's right-hand side. This is the hand the player uses to strum or pick the strings, and to control the guitar's volume and tone knobs. (The opposite holds true for left-handed players). The six strings of the guitar are threaded through the body and over the **bridge**, where each string rests on a **saddle**. The **neck** of the guitar extends from the body across the player's left side (or, again, over the opposite side for left-handed players). The front-facing side of the neck, known as the **fretboard**, is divided into different spaces by small metal dividers known as **frets**. The spaces are in some ways similar to the keys on a piano: as the player presses down on these spaces with left hand and plucks the corresponding strings with the right hand, different notes are produced. As the neck extends away from the body of the guitar, the spaces between the frets get wider and wider, and the pitches produced by pressing down on them gets lower and lower. The fretboard ends at the **head** of the guitar, where the strings are wound into **tuning pegs**.

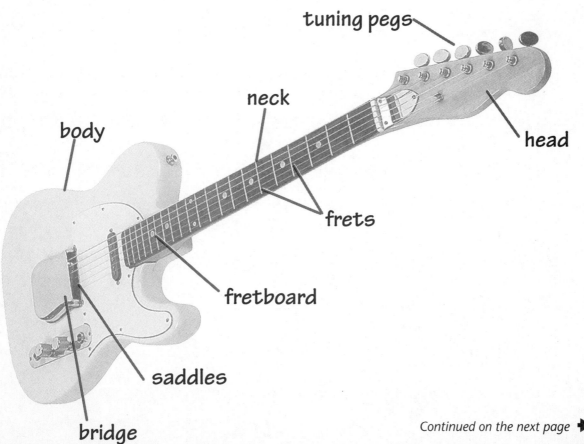

Continued on the next page ➤

Continued from the previous page

In many ways, the term "electric guitar" is something of a misnomer; unlike other electronic devices, the "electric" guitar does not actually run on electricity. It might be more appropriate to refer to the instrument as the "electromagnetic" guitar, since this is the force that allows the instrument to produce sound. The body of every electric guitar is fitted with one or more **pickups**, which are located under the strings between the bridge and the neck. These pickups are made up of six small magnetic rods—one beneath each string—wrapped together with as many as 7,000 turns of fine wire. The pickups create a small magnetic field through which the metal strings of the guitar pass. When the player strums the strings, they vibrate, and this vibration causes a vibration in the magnetic field, which then creates a vibrating current charge in the coiled wire. The pickup's coil then sends this electrical signal to a volume knob, which controls the amount of signal that reaches the guitar's **output jack**. Most guitars do not have an internal power source, so on its own this signal is very small. In order for an electric guitar to produce enough sound to be clearly audible, a cable must be connected to the guitar's input jack. This cable is then connected to an **amplifier**, which boosts the original charge enough to move a speaker, which then converts the electric signal into sound.

Answer these questions about "The Electric Guitar." Write your answers in complete sentences.

1. How is the meaning of the word *fret* as it is used in the passage different from the definition of the word when it is used as a verb?

_____

_____

2. Why do you think the magnets referred to in the passage are known as *pickups*?

_____

_____

3. Consider the names of the different parts of the guitar—*body*, *neck*, and *head*. Considering the literal definitions of these words, why are these names appropriate?

_____

_____

4. Why do you think the saddles described in the passage are referred to by that term?

_____

_____

Author's Purpose and Point of View

Learn About It

The **purpose** of writing nonfiction is to inform, persuade, or entertain. **Informational passages** present a series of facts or observations to the reader. **Persuasive essays** are designed to influence a reader's thinking about a particular topic. Authors can persuade readers by supporting their **views** with evidence, or by pointing out how their opponent's views are flawed. Many authors actually strengthen their arguments by acknowledging and refuting the claims of those with opposing points of view. Passages that are designed to entertain tell a story or describe a person or scene.

Read the passage. As you read, try to determine the author's purpose for writing the passage.

A number of parents in our district argue that children should be allowed to keep cell phones in school for security reasons. While this is a valid concern, recent research shows that cell phones do more harm than good. Nearly one-third of all high school students have admitted to using cell phones to cheat on tests. What's more, cell phones have become yet another tool that bullies use to prey on weaker students.

Main Idea	Point of View	Author's Purpose
Cell phones do more harm than good.	Students cheat on tests. Bullies prey on weaker students.	To persuade

Try It

Read the passage. As you read, try to identify the author's purpose and point of view. Underline the sentences that help you identify the point of view. Use the questions to help you.

Argument Against High-Speed Rail Systems

Over the past few years, a number of commentators have been clamoring for the development of a high-speed rail system in our state. The main reasoning behind this initiative seems to amount to little more than an international game of keeping up with the Joneses: "Other industrialized nations have high-speed rail, so we should have it, too!" Supporters breathlessly tout the advantages of a system that would allow commuters to travel from Los Angeles to San Francisco in under two-and-a-half hours, forgetting that such a mode of transportation already exists—it is called *an airplane*. When one weighs the negligible rewards yielded by such a system against the enormous financial and environmental toll it would take, the choice is clear. A high-speed rail system is an intriguing idea, but it is one whose time has not yet come.

> What was the author's purpose for writing this passage?

Proponents of the proposed rail system point to the fact that its construction would create thousands of new jobs for our state's unemployed workers. Unfortunately, these gains would only be in the short term, and would be offset by the intense strain that construction costs would put on our state's finances. Even by conservative estimates, the cost of implementing such a system would be over $40 billion, at a time when the state budget is already stretched to the limit. Over the last year, the state legislature has been forced to make drastic cuts to education, police and fire departments, and social services. How much more will taxpayers be expected to suffer to enable a small group of commuters to get where they're going *slightly* faster than they did before?

> Is this an informational passage or a persuasive essay? How can you tell?

Continued on the next page ➤

Continued from the previous page

Some environmental activists claim that the increased efficiency of the proposed system would encourage more people to use mass transportation, resulting in reduced emissions levels and less pollution. These activists fail to consider the profoundly negative impact its construction would have on our state's already polluted atmosphere. The heavy machinery used to build the necessary structures, combined with the high volume of truck traffic necessary to deliver materials to job sites, would result in a pronounced spike in emission levels each year that construction continues— and who knows how long such a project might take? Construction would also lead to a disruption of current train schedules, and, in some areas, a closure of important roadways. This would lead to increased congestion on our highways, which would in turn lead to even more pollution.

Does the author present an alternate opinion to the proposed project?

Instead of squandering a lot of time, treasure, and trouble on what amounts to a glorified monorail system, it would be better for us to focus on developing our infrastructure on a more local level. This could be done most effectively by constructing light rail systems, maintaining bridges, and improving our current highways. Such measures would add jobs, ease congestion, and reduce emissions without putting undue strain on our already beleaguered economy.

HOTS **Evaluate**

How does the author of this passage use the point of view of her opponents to strengthen her own argument?

Apply It

Read the passage. As you read, try to identify the author's purpose and point of view. Answer the questions that follow.

Wind Energy

Perhaps the most pressing challenge we face in the twenty-first century is the need to develop sustainable, renewable energy sources to meet the ever-increasing demands of our technology-based society. Currently, we depend on fossil fuels to meet most of our energy needs, from fueling our cars to powering our larger electrical plants. As their supply has become more and more limited, the cost of producing such fuels has risen dramatically, as has the environmental damage caused by their continued use. Since the majority of the world's oil is produced in politically unstable regions, many countries are beginning to view the search for low-cost, "green" energy alternatives, not just as an urgent economic concern, but as a matter of national security as well.

One of the most promising alternatives to fossil fuels is also one of the most ancient: wind power. Like its primitive cousin, the windmill, the modern wind turbine has the potential to generate a great deal of power at a negligible cost. Unlike fossil fuels or nuclear energy, wind power produces no toxic by-products, so the installation and operation of wind turbines has little or no negative effect on the environment. What's more, these turbines have proven to be much more adaptable than other power-generating structures. Since each wind turbine occupies only a few square meters and is relatively easy to construct, turbines have the potential to be a great source of energy for remote locations such as mountainous regions and rural areas. With such a small footprint, these turbines also leave the land surrounding them open to other productive applications, such as agriculture or irrigation. Given all of these advantages, wind power is the cheapest and safest energy resource for developing countries, and increased investment in its application would spur the growth of new businesses in industrialized nations.

Continued on the next page ➤

Continued from the previous page

Critics of wind power might argue that generating energy from wind power is about as reliable as the weather itself—that is, not at all. In some areas, the wind force might not be consistent enough to keep the turbines turning on a regular basis. But no one is arguing that wind power is some sort of magical cure-all that can solve our energy problems in one bold stroke. Even fossil fuels, omnipresent though they might seem, need to be supplemented by other sources to meet today's high demand for energy. Similarly, coupling wind energy with other low-cost, environment-friendly energy sources such as solar power should do more than enough to overcome any of wind power's perceived shortcomings.

The other arguments against wind power are of the more superficial variety: that fields of wind turbines mar the landscape, that the turbines are noisy, etc. But isn't a field of gently spinning, symmetrical windmills more appealing than the sight of a chugging oil refinery? Or a coal mine? Or a nuclear plant? And as far as the noise pollution, what is a little ambient noise compared to the pollution and environmental damage wrought by fossil fuel energy? Compared to the innumerable benefits of wind energy, it seems a small price to pay.

Answer these questions about "Wind Energy." Write your answers in complete sentences.

1. What was the author's purpose in writing this passage?

_____

_____

2. What type of passage is this? How can you tell?

_____

_____

3. What is the function of the first paragraph in regard to the author's overall argument?

_____

_____

4. How does the author support his argument in the second paragraph?

_____

_____

5. How does the author respond to the potential shortcomings of wind power?

_____

_____

6. How does the author respond to critics in the final paragraph?

_____

_____

Word Choice and Tone

Learn About It

Tone refers to an author's attitude to a particular subject or audience. It is displayed through the author's **word choice**, as well as through the style and structure of the passage. The tone of a nonfiction passage can be serious or humorous, formal or informal. Serious or formal passages will feature language that is usually straightforward, direct, and official, while humorous or informal passages are often more conversational, creative, and playful.

Read the party invitations. As you read, pay attention to each author's word choice, and think about how this reflects the author's tone.

You are cordially invited to the birthday celebration of **Edward West** to be held on Thursday, August 3rd. Refreshments will be served. Please RSVP at your earliest convenience.	Hey guys! Come check out my **Beach Barbecue Birthday Bash**! It's gonna be a blast! Munchies, music, fun! Be there or be square! (Pass it on…)

Formal Tone	Informal Tone
Official, serious language	Conversational language, slang
Straightforward, direct	Figurative language, creative expressions
Reflects respectful, distant relationship to audience	Reflects casual, familiar relationship to audience

Try It

Read the passage. As you read, circle the words that reflect the author's tone. Use the questions to help you.

excerpted and adapted from

The Boston Cooking-School Cook Book
by Fannie Farmer

The principal ways of cooking are boiling, broiling, stewing, roasting, baking, and frying. Boiling is cooking in boiling water. Solid food so cooked is called boiled food, though literally this expression is incorrect. Examples: boiled eggs, potatoes, mutton, etc.

Water boils at 212°F (sea level), and simmers at 185°F. Slowly boiling water has the same temperature as rapidly boiling water, and consequently is able to do the same work.

Watery vapor and steam pass off from boiling water. Steam is invisible; watery vapor is visible, and is often miscalled steam. Commonly used cooking utensils permit the escape of watery vapor and steam; thereby much heat is lost if food is cooked in rapidly boiling water.

> How would you describe the organization of the passage?

> Does the passage strike you as humorous in any way? Or is the passage conversational?

Water is boiled for two purposes: first, cooking of itself to destroy organic impurities; second, for cooking foods. Boiling water toughens and hardens albumen in eggs; toughens fibrin, and dissolves tissues in meat; bursts starch-grains, and softens cellulose in cereals and vegetables. Milk should never be allowed to boil. At boiling temperature (214°F), the casein is slightly hardened, and the fat is rendered more difficult of digestion. Milk heated over boiling water, as in a double boiler, is called scalded milk, and reaches a temperature of 196°F. When foods are cooked over hot water, the process is called steaming.

Continued on the next page ➤

Continued from the previous page

Broiling is cooking over or in front of a clear fire. The food to be cooked is usually placed in a greased broiler or on a gridiron held near the coals, turned often at first to sear the outside—thus preventing escape of inner juices—afterwards turned occasionally. Tender meats and fish may be cooked in this way. The flavor obtained by broiling is particularly fine; there is, however, a greater loss of weight in this than in any other way of cooking, as the food thus cooked is exposed to free circulation of air.

Stewing is cooking in a small amount of hot water for a long time at low temperature; it is the most economical way of cooking meats, as all nutriment is retained, and the ordinary way of cooking cheaper cuts. Thus fibers and connective tissues are softened, and the whole is made tender and palatable.

Roasting is cooking before a clear fire, with a reflector to concentrate the heat. Heat is applied in the same way as for broiling, the difference being that the meat for roasting is placed on a spit and allowed to revolve, thicker pieces always being employed. Meats cooked in a range oven, though really baked, are said to be roasted.

Baking is cooking in a range oven.

Frying is cooking by means of immersion in deep fat raised to a temperature of 350° to 400°F.

> Note the words the author uses. How does this word choice affect the tone?

HOTS Analyze

How does the author's word choice affect the tone of the passage?

Apply It

Read the passage. As you read, think about how the author's word choice affects the tone of the passage. Answer the questions that follow.

Rockin' Guacamole

You might now know this, but I'm kind of famous. Well, maybe I'm not famous, but my Rockin' Guacamole recipe sure is. My "guac" is so famous, in fact, that it gets invited to parties before I do. People have been known to come to blows over the last spoonful. OK, maybe I'm exaggerating a bit there, but I always make sure to make a little extra just to be on the safe side. See, on the West Coast we take our guacamole pretty seriously, and I've been working on perfecting my recipe for years now. From what hundreds of satisfied "customers" have told me, I'm pretty sure I have it down.

The key to making Rockin' Guacamole is, of course, using only fresh avocados. (Fun fact: avocados are also referred to as *alligator pears*, since the color and texture of their skin makes them look like alligators. Just thought you might like to know.) The great thing about avocados is that they not only taste great, but they're also really good for you. They're really rich in potassium, which apparently is really good for your heart or something like that. You know what else they're really good for? Chips and burgers. But I digress…

Anyway, aside from about five avocados, here's all you need (as in, DON'T add anything else): cilantro, chopped onion, chopped tomatoes, pepper, fresh lime juice, and salt.

Continued on the next page ▶

Continued from the previous page

So here's what you do: cut the avocados in half and get rid of the pit. Scoop out the insides and place them in a bowl. Squeeze in the fresh lime juice, and then mash it all together. Don't mash it up, too much, though—you want the guac to be really thick, not runny. Once you're done with that, throw in the other ingredients, and give it one more mash. Add salt to taste, give it one more mash, and you're ready to rock.

Here are those ingredients again. Feel free to experiment with the amount of each, but I've found that this is what works best:

> 5 perfectly ripe avocados
> 1 or 2 limes, squeezed
> minced onion
> 1/3 cup chopped cilantro
> 2 chopped plum tomatoes
> 1/4 teaspoon ground pepper
> salt to taste

Serve with fresh tortilla chips, or spread on your favorite burger. Rock out!

Answer these questions about "Rockin' Guacamole." Write your answers in complete sentences.

1. What sort of relationship does the author of this passage have with his audience?

_____

_____

2. Do you see any evidence of humor in this passage? Where?

_____

_____

3. Do you notice any use of slang or conversational language in this passage?

_____

_____

4. Based on your answers to the previous questions, how would you describe the tone of this passage?

_____

_____

Paragraph Structure

Learn About It

Most **paragraphs** in a work of nonfiction are made up of three types of sentences. The **topic sentence** contains the main idea of the paragraph. Although not always the first sentence, the topic sentence is usually placed at the beginning of a paragraph. The topic sentence is usually followed by a series of **supporting details**, or **examples** that support the main idea. **Transitional sentences** can introduce links to other paragraphs, indicate a shift in the author's argument, or state the conclusion of the paragraph.

Read the paragraph. As you read, try to identify what role each sentence plays in the paragraph.

Jackie Robinson is one of the most important sports figures of the twentieth century. As the first African American to play major league baseball, Robinson brought the issue of civil rights to the forefront of American life. His success as a ballplayer broke down barriers for an entire generation of African American athletes. However, his triumphs extended to the world beyond the ball field as well.

Parts of a Paragraph	
Topic Sentence	Jackie Robinson is one of the most important sports figures of the twentieth century.
Supporting Details	As the first African American to play major league baseball, Robinson brought the issue of civil rights to the forefront of American life. His success as a ballplayer broke down barriers for an entire generation of African American athletes.
Transitional Sentence	However, his triumphs extended to the world beyond the ball field as well.

Try It

Read the passage. As you read, underline the topic sentence and circle the supporting details of each paragraph. Use the questions to help you.

excerpted and adapted from

Common Sense
by Thomas Paine

As much has been said of the advantages of reconciliation, which, like an agreeable dream, has passed away and left us as we were, it is but right that we should examine the opposing side of the argument, and inquire into some of the many material injuries which these colonies sustain, and always will sustain, by being connected with and dependent on Great Britain.

I have heard it asserted by some that as America has flourished under her former connection with Great Britain, the same connection is necessary toward her future happiness. Nothing can be more untrue than this kind of argument. We may as well assert that because a child has thrived upon milk, that it is never to have meat, or that the first twenty years of our lives is to become a precedent for the next twenty. But even this is admitting more than is true; for I answer roundly that America would have flourished as much, and probably much more, had no European power taken any notice of her. The commerce by which she has enriched herself are the necessaries of life, and will always have a market while eating is the custom of Europe.

What is the role of the first sentence of this passage?

Continued on the next page ➤

Continued from the previous page

But she has protected us, say some. That she has engrossed us is true, and defended the continent at our expense as well as her own, is admitted; and she would have defended Turkey from the same motive: that is, for the sake of trade and dominion.

> Pay attention to the topic sentences of the third and fourth paragraphs. What role do these sentences play in Paine's overall argument?

But Britain is the parent country, say some. Then the more shame upon her conduct. Even brutes do not devour their young, nor savages make war upon their families. Why, the assertion, if true, turns to her blame. Europe, and not England, is the parent country of America. This New World has been the asylum for the persecuted lovers of civil and religious liberty from EVERY PART of Europe. Here have they fled, not from the tender embraces of the mother, but from the cruelty of the monster; and it is so far true of England, that the same tyranny which drove the first emigrants from home, pursues their descendents still. We claim brotherhood with every European, and triumph in the generosity of the sentiment.

But, admitting that we were all of English descent, what does it amount to? Nothing. Britain, being now an open enemy, extinguishes every other name and title: and to say that reconciliation is our duty is truly farcical. The first king of England, of the present line (William the Conqueror) was a Frenchman, and half the peers of England are descendants from the same country; why, by the same method of reasoning, England ought to be governed by France.

> Which transitional words does the author use? How do these words help connect different ideas?

Do you think Paine effectively supports his topic sentences?

Apply It

Read the passage. As you read, pay attention to the structure of each paragraph. Answer the questions that follow.

Yoga

In recent years, yoga has become one of the most popular forms of physical and spiritual exercise in the United States, with over 16 million regular practitioners. Despite its popularity, relatively few Americans have a clear idea of what yoga is all about. Many think of it as merely another form of alternative medicine, the latest low-impact exercise fad, or as some sort of New Age pseudo-religion. Yet yoga is far from new. In fact, in many ways its practice is as old as civilization itself: artifacts dating as far back as 3000 BCE depict figures in positions resembling modern yoga poses. The term *yoga* itself is derived from the ancient Sanskrit language, and is perceived to have many different meanings. For the sake of convenience, it would be best to define the term *yoga* as meaning "union," since its aim is achieving harmony and balance between a person's mind, body, and spirit.

To the casual observer, yoga might look like little more than stretching. These physical postures, known as *asana*, are just one aspect of the eight "limbs" of yoga, though they form the bulk of yoga as it is practiced by most of its adherents in the United States. The aim of these postures is to develop the structure of the body by aligning the vertebrae, increasing flexibility, and strengthening muscles. Such poses have also been shown to benefit the functioning of internal organs, detoxify the body, and stimulate and nourish the brain and central nervous system. Another aspect that attracts people to yoga is that the postures can be practiced in a manner that most benefits the practitioner. They can be performed slowly to increase stamina and perfect the execution of the pose, or they can be done in rapid succession as a form or aerobic exercise. Whatever the pace, the goal of the postures is to prepare the body for the breathing, cleansing, and meditation practices that make up the rest of the practice of yoga.

Continued on the next page ➤

Continued from the previous page

There are numerous benefits to practicing yoga regularly. Even after just a few lessons with a qualified instructor, most newcomers to yoga experience a sharper mental focus and a greater sense of overall well-being. Proper yoga practice has also been shown to improve digestion, build immunity from common diseases, and help practitioners overcome chronic pain and injuries. In some cases, yoga has also been shown to help children overcome physical or developmental disabilities. Children with learning disabilities or behavioral disorders who practice yoga regularly have been shown to develop better concentration, poise, and emotional stability.

It should be stressed that, in spite of the fact that some of its results can be felt almost immediately, yoga is not a "quick fix." Like any form of exercise, yoga is most effective when it is learned gradually and practiced regularly under the guidance of a qualified instructor. When studied with patience and dedication, yoga can yield benefits that last a lifetime.

Answer these questions about "Yoga." Write your answers in complete sentences.

1. What role does the sentence "Many think of it as merely another form of alternative medicine" play in the first paragraph?

_____

_____

2. Notice that the fourth sentence of the first paragraph begins with the word *yet*. What does this indicate about the information that follows?

_____

_____

3. What type of sentence is "To the casual observer, yoga might look like little more than stretching"?

_____

_____

4. How do the other sentences in the second paragraph relate to the topic sentence?

_____

_____

5. Describe the structure of the third paragraph in your own words.

_____

_____

Author's Argument, Claims, and Evidence

Learn About It

Any **argument** or **claim** made by an author in a text must be supported by **evidence**. This evidence can come in a variety of forms, such as statistics, quotes, historical data, or personal experience. In order for this evidence to reinforce an author's argument, it must be factual, accurate, and relevant to the topic.

Read the passage. As you read, pay attention to how the author uses evidence to back up the argument in the passage, and try to identify any irrelevant evidence.

The Beatles are the most successful recording artists of all time. By some estimates, they have sold over one billion albums, and no other artist has been awarded more gold or platinum records. They have more number one singles than any artist in recording history. On top of that, they are my brother's favorite band, and he really knows what he's talking about because he plays the piano.

Evaluating an Argument	
Claim	The Beatles are the most successful artists of all time.
Relevant evidence	One billion albums were sold.
	Most were gold and platinum records.
	Most were number one singles.
Irrelevant evidence	They are my brother's favorite band.
	My brother plays the piano.

Try It

Read the passage. As you read, circle the sentences that state the author's argument. Underline the sentences that support the argument. Use the questions to help you.

Before the 19th Amendment was ratified in 1920, American women did not have the right to vote. In 1872, women's rights activist Susan B. Anthony was arrested for attempting to cast a vote in that year's presidential election. The following is a speech she gave in her own defense.

Friends and fellow citizens: I stand before you tonight under indictment for the alleged crime of having voted at the last presidential election, without having a lawful right to vote. It shall be my work this evening to prove to you that in thus voting, I simply exercised my citizen's rights, guaranteed to me and all United States citizens by the national Constitution, beyond the power of any state to deny.

The preamble of the federal Constitution says: "We, the people of the United States, in order to form a more perfect union, establish justice, insure domestic tranquility, provide for the common defense, promote the general welfare, and secure the blessings of liberty to ourselves and our posterity, do ordain and establish this Constitution for the United States of America."

It was we, the people; not we, the white male citizens; nor yet we, the male citizens; but we, the whole people, who formed the Union. And we formed it, not to give the blessings of liberty, but to secure them; not to the half of ourselves and the half of our posterity, but to the whole people—women as well as men. And it is a downright mockery to talk to women of their enjoyment of the blessings of liberty while they are denied the use of the only means of securing them provided by this democratic-republican government—the ballot.

For any state to make gender a qualification that must ever result in the disfranchisement of one entire half of the people, and is therefore a violation of the supreme law of the land. By it the blessings of liberty are forever withheld from women and their female posterity.

> **What is Anthony's argument in the passage?**

> **How does Anthony use the Constitution to support her argument?**

Continued on the next page ➡

Continued from the previous page

To them this government has no just powers derived from the consent of the governed. To them this government is not a democracy. It is an aristocracy; a hateful oligarchy of gender; the most hateful aristocracy ever established on the face of the globe; an oligarchy of wealth, where the rich govern the poor. An oligarchy of learning, where the educated govern the ignorant, or even an oligarchy of race, where the Saxon rules the African, might be endured; but this oligarchy of gender, which makes the husbands and sons the rulers over the wives and daughters of every household—which ordains all men sovereigns, all women subjects, carries dissension, discord, and rebellion into every home of the nation.

Webster, Worcester, and Bouvier all define a citizen to be a person in the United States, entitled to vote and hold office.

The only question left to be settled now is: Are women persons? I hardly believe any of our opponents will have the hardihood to say they are not. Being persons, then, women are citizens; and no state has a right to make any law, or to enforce any law, that shall abridge their rights. Hence, every discrimination against women in the constitutions and laws of the several states is today null and void.

> **How does Anthony use the definition of the word *citizen* to support her argument?**

HOTS Evaluate

Anthony claims that there are some oligarchies that "might be endured." Could this statement actually *weaken* her argument? How?

Apply It

Read the passage. As you read, pay attention to the author's use of evidence and try to determine if the evidence is relevant to the argument presented. Answer the questions that follow.

Tigers

Tigers are one of the most endangered species in the world, and their numbers are decreasing every day. Originally, eight subspecies of tigers roamed hungrily through the jungles of Asia and the area known as Eurasia, which includes parts of Russia. They were among the world's most aggressive predators. Three subspecies of tigers became extinct during the twentieth century, so now only five remain. The Bengal tiger of India is the most populous of all the world's tigers, numbering between 3,100 and 4,700.

Tigers may someday vanish from the earth entirely. In fact, the number of tigers in existence today is estimated to be somewhere between 5,000 and 7,500. First and foremost, tiger habitats are shrinking. Tigers are solitary animals, and each cat must have its own territory in which to live and hunt. Wild tigers still exist today in the jungles and forests of many Asian countries. The majority of these surviving tigers live in India. Unfortunately, the increasing human population in many Asian countries is taking over the tigers' habitats, so there are fewer areas for tigers to live. In some areas, jungles and forests inhabited by tigers are being cut and cleared to provide living space for humans. Some former tiger habitats have become logging plantations. In other areas, former tiger territory has given way to rubber plantations and various mining operations. As the forests are cleared, animals which might have been tigers' prey clear out. In short, tigers are losing their homes and their food because of the increase in human population in their native areas.

While tigers are worth saving for their beauty alone, there are other reasons for protecting them. The extinction of a carnivore like a tiger can have a drastic effect on Earth's ecosystem. When such a carnivore is removed from an area, the herbivores it preys upon can increase at a rapid rate, causing great damage to plant species.

Continued on the next page ▶

Continued from the previous page

The loss of one species basically sets a destructive cycle in motion, which affects all other species. At this point, you may be wondering why world governments are not taking steps to prevent the extinction of these magnificent animals. The fact is, governments are taking many actions to save the tigers. But are these measures enough? Refuges and preserves, where tigers can roam free from fear of being hunted or crowded out of their homes, are set aside in most of the countries where tigers live. The Indian government has taken significant steps toward setting aside such areas, but poachers have still managed to trap and kill many tigers inside these reserves.

Encroachment by the human population is also a problem which has no easy solution. Tigers cannot live comfortably in small spaces. Some experts estimate that a sole male tiger needs twenty-five miles of territory alone! Food is now in such short supply for tigers that they are hunting the domestic animals humans rely on for food. They will sometimes attack people, as well. People who feel threatened by the presence of tigers often trap, poison, or shoot the offending cats. Sadly, in some parts of the world, tigers are killed for food—or for their beautiful coats. Various tiger body parts are also used for traditional medicines throughout Asia. If tigers are to be saved, a number of other factors must be taken into consideration.

For example, poachers would not hunt tigers unless there was an economic incentive. Many experts believe tiger poaching would cease entirely if good-paying jobs existed in tiger hunting regions. Most poachers currently only get a small percentage of the market price for tiger parts. Education is another big factor in protecting tigers. If people knew about the dangers faced by these beautiful animals, they would be more likely to help protect them. So far, the most effective means of saving the tigers has been to protect wildlife reserves.

In 1973, the World Wildlife Fund, along with the country of India, started Project Tiger, a program designed to save tiger habitats. Through this program, India has designated over 500 protected national preserves, sanctuaries, and parks for the tigers. As the World Wildlife Fund points out, this affects still less than four percent of an area with a human population of over 800 million! Similar programs have been started in Nepal, Thailand, and Indonesia. If these big cats are to be saved, world governments must continue working together to protect them.

Answer these questions about "Tigers." Write your answers in complete sentences.

1. What is the author's argument in the passage?

_____

_____

2. What kind of evidence does the author give to support his argument?

_____

_____

3. What has happened to some former tiger habitats?

_____

_____

4. What does the author think about India's response to the declining tiger population?

_____

_____

5. What does the author think can help bring an end to tiger poaching?

_____

_____

Advantages and Disadvantages of Different Media

Learn About It

The **medium** through which an author chooses to express a message can have a profound effect upon how the message is received by the audience. **Print** media are the most detailed way to convey a message. Media that incorporate **video** and **audio** exhibit facial expressions, gestures, body movements, and vocal inflections.

Read the passage. As you read, think about how different media affect the way an audience interprets information.

Judging from attendance figures published by the local soccer team, one would think that the sport is now more popular than ever. One look at television coverage of the last game, however, reveals something else: the stands look almost empty.

Medium	Advantages	Disadvantages
Print (books, essays, newspaper articles)	Most detailed Not constrained by time limits Relatively inexpensive	Not as direct or immediate as video or audio Takes time to produce Does not allow audience to utilize other senses
Audio (radio, audiobooks, podcasts)	Incorporates sound Allows participants to communicate through vocal inflection	Does not incorporate visuals Not as detailed Constrained by time limits Usually more expensive to produce
Video (television, Internet)	Incorporates sound and visuals Allows participants to communicate through facial expressions, gestures, and body movement	Message is often overshadowed by presentation Not as detailed Constrained by time limits Usually more expensive to produce

Try It

Read the passage. As you read, pay attention to how the characteristics of print media affect your judgment of the events described. Use the questions to help you.

The 1960 presidential election between Republican Vice President Richard Nixon and Democratic Senator John F. Kennedy featured the first presidential debates to be broadcast live on television. The passage below is an excerpt from the transcript of the first debate, which was held on September 26, 1960.

MODERATOR: Mr. Vice President, your campaign stresses the value of your eight-year experience. Would you tell us please specifically what major proposals you have made in the last eight years that have been adopted by the administration?

> When viewed in print, how effective is Mr. Nixon's response?

MR. NIXON: First, after each of my foreign trips, I have made recommendations that have been adopted. For example, after my first trip abroad—abroad, I strongly recommended that we increase our exchange programs particularly as they related to exchange of persons of leaders in the labor field and in the information field. After my trip to South America, I made recommendations that a lending agency be set up which the South American much better than a lend—than to participate in the lending agencies which treated all the countries of the world the same. After my trip abroad to Hungary, I made some recommendations with regard to the Hungarian refugee situation which were adopted, not only by the president but some of them were enacted into law by the Congress. Within the administration, as a chairman of the President's Committee on Price Stability and Economic Growth, I have had the opportunity to make recommendations which have been adopted within the administration and which I think have been reasonably effective. I know Senator Kennedy suggested in a speech yesterday that that committee had not been particularly effective. I would only suggest that since that committee has been formed, the price line has been held very well within the United States.

Continued on the next page ➤

Continued from the previous page

MR. KENNEDY: Well, I would say in the latter that the—and that's what I found uh—somewhat unsatisfactory about the figures uh—Mr. Nixon, that you used in your previous speech, when you talked about the Truman Administration. You—Mr. Truman came to office in nineteen uh—forty-four and at the end of the war, and uh—difficulties that were facing the United States during that period of transition—1946 when price controls were lifted—so it's rather difficult to use an overall figure taking those seven and a half years and comparing them to the last eight years. In regard to uh—price stability uh—I'm not aware that that committee did produce recommendations that ever were certainly before the Congress from the point of view of legislation in regard to controlling prices. In regard to the exchange of students and labor unions, I am chairman of the subcommittee on Africa, and I think that one of the most unfortunate phases of our policy towards that country was the very minute number of exchanges that we had. I think it's true of Latin America also. We did come forward with a program of students for the Congo of over three hundred which was more than the federal government had for all of Africa the previous year, so that I don't think that uh—we have moved at least in those two areas with sufficient vigor.

Notice that the transcript of Mr. Kennedy's response includes a number of *uhs* and other pauses. How does this make you feel about his performance in the debate?

How might your judgment of this debate be affected if you were actually able to see and hear the candidates speaking?

Apply It

Read the passage. As you read, think about how changes in media affected the way the events described were perceived. Answer the questions that follow.

The passage below is an analysis of the television coverage of the debate mentioned in the previous passage, and the effect this coverage had on the outcome of the election.

The Kennedy-Nixon Election

September 26, 1960, marks a turning point not only in the history of television, but in the history of American politics as well. On that date, over 70 million viewers tuned in to watch the first in a series of televised debates between Vice President Richard Nixon and Senator John F. Kennedy. For the first time in history, American voters were given a chance to see their candidates in action, and as a result, were able to judge their performance not just on the words they spoke, but how they appeared as they spoke them. Before the debates, Nixon and Kennedy were viewed as equals in both style and substance. Many experts gave Nixon the edge in terms of experience and campaigning ability, and polls taken before the first debate gave him a slim lead over his Democratic opponent. The way that they projected on television, however, presented a pronounced contrast to American voters, a contrast that ultimately benefited Kennedy when the final election results were tallied in November.

In the months leading up to the first debate, Nixon had promised, against the counsel of his advisors, to campaign in all fifty states. Unfortunately, in the course of that campaigning, he seriously injured his knee, and was hospitalized for two weeks in August. Barely recovered, he resumed his grueling schedule, campaigning all the way up until the day of the debate itself. Kennedy, by contrast, maintained a relatively light schedule in sunny California. Unlike Nixon, Kennedy and his advisors engaged in painstaking preparations for the debate, reviewing such minute details as how to sit, what suit to wear, and how to carry himself when he was not speaking.

Continued on the next page ➤

Continued from the previous page

The results of the candidates' respective efforts were glaringly obvious on camera. Nixon, still recovering from his injury and a bout with the flu, appeared painfully frail and thin. He refused to wear makeup for the debate; as a result, his perspiration was clearly visible, and his pale complexion and beard stubble made him appear tired and haggard. His grey suit, which blended in with the studio backdrop, added to his ghostly pallor. Meanwhile, Kennedy, who previously had a reputation for being sickly, looked the very picture of health—tanned, youthful, and relaxed. To the millions of viewers watching the debate in their homes, Kennedy projected calm, confidence, and youthful vigor, while Nixon came across as anxious, uncertain, and uncomfortable.

The effect these images had on the voters who were watching was striking. Studies conducted after the debates found that the telegenic Kennedy's charisma made him the clear winner in the minds of television viewers. By contrast, those who had listened to the debates on the radio gave the edge to Nixon, as did most members of the print media who were covering the event in person. Kennedy's subsequent triumph in November sent a clear message to future aspirants to the Presidency: one's image is just as important as (and, indeed, perhaps more important than) one's message.

Answer these questions about "The Kennedy-Nixon Election." Write your answers in complete sentences.

1. According to this passage, how was Kennedy able to use the medium of television to his advantage?

   _____

   _____

2. What impression did Kennedy's appearance make on voters?

   _____

   _____

3. How would this impression of Kennedy have been different if coverage of the debate were limited to just a transcript?

   _____

   _____

4. Notice that radio listeners judged the debate in favor of Nixon. What does this tell you about Nixon's speaking performance?

   _____

   _____

5. Many newspaper accounts also gave the edge to Nixon. What does this tell you about the details of each candidate's message?

   _____

   _____

6. Why do you think it was important to voters for a prospective president to look confident, relaxed, and healthy?

   _____

   _____

Analyze Conflicting Information in Two Texts

Learn About It

> In many cases, two texts will present **conflicting information** about the same topic. When **comparing** these competing claims, it is important to **evaluate** the **evidence** used by each author. **Arguments** based on bias, personal attacks, or opinions are considered weak. On the other hand, arguments based on evidence such as scientific data, mathematical reasoning, or primary documents tend to be much stronger.

Read the passages. As you read, pay attention to how the authors support their arguments.

AUTHOR 1: Those who argue that Earth revolves around the sun are obviously wrong. After all, all you have to do is watch how the sun moves in the sky during the day to know that it is actually the sun that revolves around Earth.

AUTHOR 2: Actually, by observing the motion of the stars and using simple geometry, scientists have known that the sun is the center of the solar system for centuries. Their findings have been confirmed by data collected from numerous space missions. The phenomenon they're describing is actually a result of Earth's revolving around the sun.

Evidence	Author 1	Author 2
During the day, the sun appears to move across the sky.	Bases judgment on appearances and appeals to common sense (This is the weaker argument.)	Bases judgment on mathematical reasoning and scientific data (This is the stronger argument.)

Try It

Read the passages. As you read, take note of the conflicting information in the two texts. Use the questions to help you.

Abner Doubleday, the Inventor of Baseball

For the greater part of the last century, Cooperstown, New York, has been recognized as the official birthplace of baseball, and since 1939 it has been the home of the National Baseball Hall of Fame and Museum. This is largely thanks to the findings of the Mills Commission, which was convened in 1905 by baseball pioneer and sporting goods magnate Albert Spalding. The commission, which was comprised of a number of sports executives and former professional players, concluded that former Civil War general Abner Doubleday first set down the rules and format of our national pastime in 1839.

> **Would Graves's testimony be more or less convincing than written evidence from Doubleday himself?**

The commission based it findings primarily on the written testimony of one Abner Graves, then a 71-year-old mining engineer living in Denver, Colorado. Graves, himself a native of Cooperstown and a former schoolmate of Doubleday, claimed to have been present when Doubleday modified a local children's game into what we now know as baseball, and also claimed to have been present at its first contest. According to Graves's account, Doubleday sketched the original layout of the modern baseball field, and defined the placement and roles of each of its position players. Almost thirty years later, an old, fragile ball believed to have belonged to Graves was unearthed in a Cooperstown farmhouse. Given the ball's age and Graves's connection to Doubleday, many concluded that the ball must have been created by Doubleday himself, and thus it was offered as further proof that Doubleday was the game's sole inventor. To this day, the ball is referred to as the "Doubleday Baseball."

> **What might make the "Doubleday Baseball" evidence more convincing?**

71

Alexander Joy Cartwright, the Inventor of Baseball

Contrary to the accepted mythology regarding baseball's beginnings, it is unlikely that the game had a single inventor, nor can it be said to have originated in a single place. The game's purported originator, Civil War hero Abner Doubleday, never himself claimed to have invented baseball, and never once mentioned the game in his exhaustive diaries. In fact, throughout his life he professed an aversion to outdoor sports of any kind. Even if he had claimed to have invented the game, such a claim could have easily been refuted by a simple fact: in 1839, when Doubleday was supposedly inventing the national pastime in Cooperstown, he was actually enrolled as a student at West Point, some 150 miles away.

If baseball does indeed have a single "father," it is more than likely Alexander Joy Cartwright, who, unlike Doubleday, is actually enshrined in baseball's Hall of Fame. In 1842, Cartwright organized New York's Knickerbocker Base Ball Club, with whom he established and formalized the rules and regulations of the modern game. Among other innovations, Cartwright is credited with drawing the first diagram of the now familiar diamond-shaped baseball field. Transcripts from the Knickerbockers' club meetings show that Cartwright officially codified the game's rules as early as 1845. The following year, Cartwright presided over the first recorded baseball contest, which was held not in Cooperstown, but at Elysian Fields in Hoboken, New Jersey. The official lineup card from that game still exists, and shows that Cartwright's Knickerbockers fell to the New York Nine by a lopsided score of 23–1.

> How does the evidence given in the first paragraph effectively refute the arguments made in the previous passage?

> How is the evidence put forward in support of Cartwright more convincing?

HOTS Evaluate

Notice that most of the evidence presented in support of Doubleday comes from Cooperstown. How might this be evidence of bias?

Apply It

Read the passages. As you read, take note of the conflicting information in the two texts. Answer the questions that follow.

The Moon Landing Was Fake

On July 20, 1969, an estimated 600 million television viewers tuned in to watch live coverage of what conventional history regards as a great milestone in human history—the touchdown of *Apollo 11*'s *Eagle* module on the lunar surface, and Neil Armstrong's subsequent moon walk. It was thereafter billed, in Armstrong's own words, as "a giant leap for mankind"—the apex of human scientific achievement, and proof of America's limitless might and boundless ingenuity. But according to a growing number of detractors, what those 600 million people watched that evening was not history in the making, but rather an elaborate hoax staged by NASA to outstrip the Soviet Union's space program and cement America's position as the world's dominant superpower. According to these conspiracy theorists, the proof of this deception lies in the very "evidence" that NASA produced (or, more appropriately, concocted) in support of its great achievement.

One of the most memorable images from this purported moon landing (and, conveniently, a great propaganda boon for the United States) was captured in the film of astronauts Neil Armstrong and Buzz Aldrin planting an American flag in the moon's surface, ostensibly "claiming" it in the name of the United States. If you look closely at

Continued on the next page ➤

Continued from the previous page

the footage, you'll notice that the flag appears to be *flapping* as Aldrin salutes it. In the vacuum of the moon's atmosphere, such a waving motion would be impossible, a fact which leads most conspiracy theorists to conclude that this scene wasn't filmed on the moon at all.

The photos supposedly taken during the Apollo mission also reveal a great deal in what they do *not* show—namely, stars. One would think that, on the moon's dark landscape, with no atmospheric interference, a multitude of stars should be visible, more than would be seen in the nighttime sky on Earth. In the photos released by NASA, however, all one sees is an ominous black backdrop. Could this be because NASA illusionists lacked the ability to replicate convincing "stars" for their elaborate production? Many theorists seem to think so.

Like latter-day sleuths, these detractors have also unearthed a number of clues from the footprints supposedly left by Armstrong and Aldrin during their moon walks. Photos taken on the "lunar surface" show that the astronauts left behind remarkably detailed footprints, of the kind that one would normally see in damp, muddy soil. The problem is, the soil on the surface is not only very fine, it is bone dry. Creating detailed boot treads in such a surface would be like trying to make footprints in talcum powder—it just is not possible.

But if the Apollo "astronauts" did not go to the moon, where exactly did they go? This is where the conspiracy theorists differ. Some say that while shots showing the Saturn rocket launch and module splashdown are authentic, the rest of the mission was the result of a Hollywood-style production, filmed on a remote sound stage mocked up to resemble the surface of the moon.

The Moon Landing Was Real

For some reason, in recent years a growing number of crackpot conspiracy theorists and armchair rocket scientists have come forward with a variety of half-baked hypotheses as to how NASA "faked" the historic *Apollo 11* moon landing in an elaborate scheme to one-up the Soviet Union. (As if Soviet scientists themselves wouldn't be able to immediately expose such a flawed cover-up, if such a cover-up existed.) Why these people would want to deprive America (and indeed, all of humankind) of one its crowning achievements is beyond me. Luckily, anyone with a basic understanding of astronomy, or even just an amateur knowledge of photography, can pick apart these theories and reveal them as the lies they are.

One of the first things the average conspiracy theorist will bring up when discussing the alleged *Apollo* hoax is the absence of stars in the numerous photographs taken during the mission. When those photographs were taken, the lunar surface was brightly illuminated by the sun, and all of the astronauts photographed were wearing white spacesuits that were also brightly lit by the sun. The cameras used had to be set to very fast exposure times to capture such bright objects. The stars in the distance, then, would have been too faint to be picked up on film. If you have ever tried to take a picture at night, you have probably encountered the same problem.

Another one of the smoking guns in the conspiracy theorists' case is the "waving" flag that Buzz Aldrin and Neil Armstrong planted on the moon's surface. "How could a flag 'wave' like that in an airless atmosphere?" they might ask. The answer is that what you're witnessing in that footage isn't the result of some phantom breeze; it is the product of simple inertia. The flag used was inserted into an upside-down "L" shaped flagpole, with a rod supporting the top as well as the side of the flag. When Aldrin and Armstrong planted this flagpole into the lunar soil, they twisted it back and forth to make sure that it stayed in place. The "flapping" that you see is the result of this twisting motion—the bracketed top portion of the flag moves first, and then the bottom of the cloth follows it. Anyone who has put a tent pole into the ground has witnessed the same reaction. No breeze is necessary to create such a motion.

Continued on the next page ➡

Continued from the previous page

Unfortunately, since most people lack the scientific knowledge to refute these claims on their own, these crazy notions have actually found a wide audience. Fortunately, the greatest proof that American astronauts actually *did* go to the moon is also the most tangible: the hundreds of pounds of moon rocks brought back from the *Apollo* missions. Anyone who has held or viewed such rocks will tell you plainly that they are unlike any form of rock they've ever encountered on Earth. The only possible explanation, then, is that these rocks were, in fact, taken from the lunar surface.

Answer these questions about "The Moon Landing Was Fake" and "The Moon Landing Was Real." Write your answers in complete sentences.

1. For the most part, both authors make use of the same evidence to support their claims. On which aspect of this evidence does the author of "The Moon Landing Was Fake" focus?

_____

_____

2. Which aspects of this evidence does the author of "The Moon Landing Was Real" focus on?

_____

_____

3. Which author's argument is more convincing? Why?

_____

_____

4. How might the author of "The Moon Landing Was Real" respond to the footprint evidence used by the author of "The Moon Landing Was Fake"?

_____

_____

5. How might the author of "The Moon Landing Was Fake" respond to the moon rock evidence used by the author of "The Moon Landing Was Real"?

_____

_____

Graphic Organizers

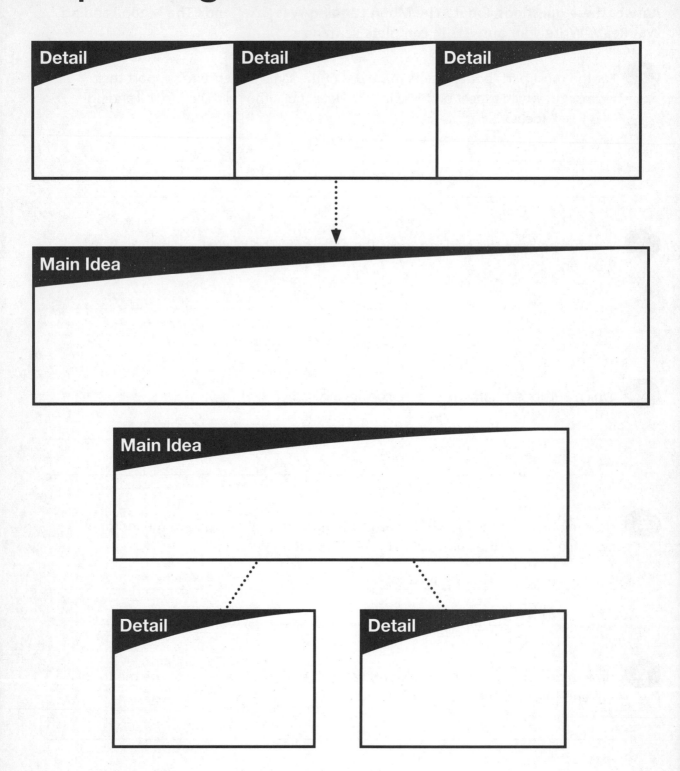

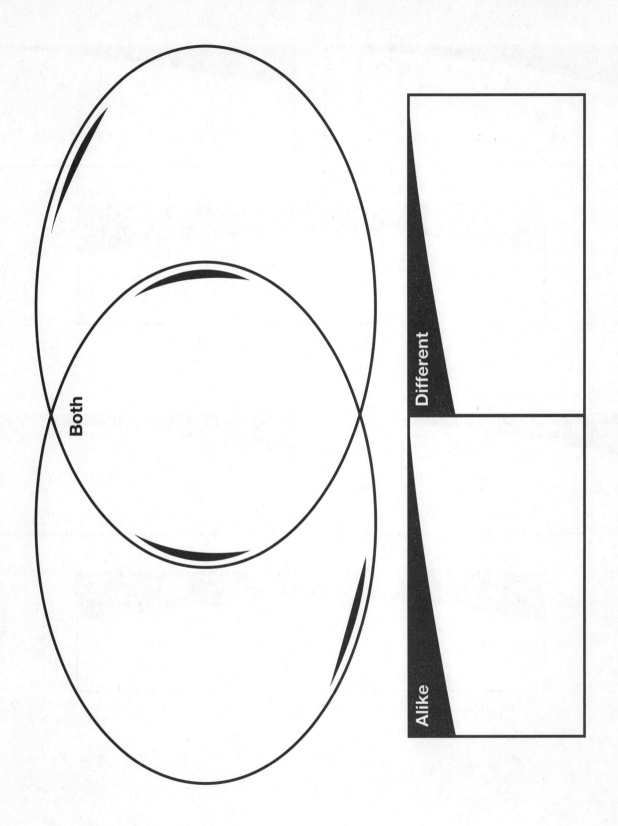

Both

Different

Alike

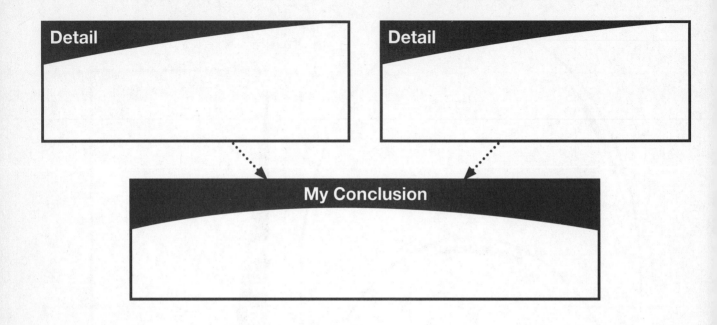

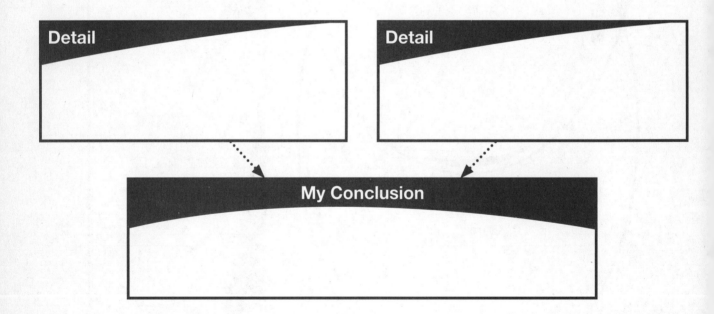